P9-EME-368

Decorate Your Doors

Decorate Your Doors

Edie Stockstill

A STERLING/CHAPELLE BOOK
Sterling Publishing Co., Inc.   New York

Owner: *Jo Packham*

Editorial: *Cathy Sexton*

Staff: *Trice Boerens, Malissa Boatwright, Rebecca Christensen, Holly Fuller, Cherie Hanson, Holly Hollingsworth, Susan Jorgensen, Amanda McPeck, Tammy Perkins, Jamie C. Pierce, Leslie Ridenour, Amy Vineyard, Nancy Whitley, and Lorrie Young.*

Photographer: *Ryne Hazen*

The photographs in this book were taken at the homes of Edie Stockstill, Jo Packham, and Ryne Hazen. We are appreciative of your time and hospitality.

Library of Congress Cataloging-in-Publication Data

Stockstill, Edie.
  Decorate your doors / Edie Stockstill.
    p. cm.
  "A Sterling / Chapelle Book"
  Includes index.
  ISBN 0-8069-0968-4
  1. Handicraft.   2. Interior decoration.   3. Doors.   I. Title.
TT857.S76   1994
747' .3—dc20   94-36664
                                                   CIP

10 9 8 7 6 5 4 3 2 1

A Sterling/Chapelle Book

Published by Sterling Publishing Company, Inc.
387 Park Avenue South, New York, N.Y. 10016
©1994 by Chapelle Ltd.
Distributed by Canada by Sterling Publishing
C/O Canadian Manda Group, One Atlantic Avenue, Suite 105
Toronto, Ontario, Canada M6K 3E7
Distributed in Great Britain and Europe by Cassell PLC
Villiers House, 41/27 Strand, London WC2N 5JE, England
Distributed in Australia by Capricorn Link (Australia) Pty Ltd.
P.O. Box 6651, Baulkham Hills, Business Centre, NSW 2153, Australia
Printed in Hong Kong
All rights reserved

Sterling ISBN 0-8069-0968-4

TABLE OF CONTENTS

A first impression is said to be indelible. What is presented at the door is the beginning of a home, a foundation for what lies beyond. As an interior designer, I feel people often miss an opportunity to enhance their homes when they overlook the entrances. Most people only see our homes from the outside, so show them something about the creativity and warmth in your home by decorating your door. Decorating a door is simple and with only a little work and creativity your decorations can express an entire feel about your home.

From a decorating standpoint, doors are easy. You can affordably and regularly change the way you decorate them to fit the seasons or your mood.

As a door invites people into your home, I invite you into my book and some of the homes which have influenced my decorative style. The first chapter deals with my memories of my husband's hometown in Branson, Missouri with its natural, country decorating style. The second chapter remembers the birthplace of my namesake, Edith Chase, in Eaglesmere, Pennsylvania with its Victorian charm and elegance. Finally, we will enter into my creative world to look at some of my favorite ways to decorate your door.

—Edie Stockstill

CHAPTER
ONE

Branson, Missouri

Branson, Missouri is the place where my husband was raised. It is where both of his parents, and generations before them, were raised. It is the place where I spent time with my husband and his family, where memories were made, and where the inspirations for the doors in this chapter were created.

Branson, was filled with doors that said "welcome" and invited guests in. And even though those doors were fairly plain and simple they were always open to anyone who wished to spend an hour or two. In this, the first chapter of my book, I used my memories from Branson to create doors that would for you, not be so plain and simple, but would be so new they had yet been undreamed of but still have that old fashioned "welcome".

My husband's grandparents, there is a picture of them on their wedding day, lived on a farm where on summer afternoons I could see dark grapes glistening in the sun. These grapes that my husband and I would pick together as the evening sun was setting were the inspiration for my Grapevine Garland and Grapevine Wreath doors.

Laundry "day" was very much a tradition with my mother-in-law and helping her with laundry day chores, listening to her stories, and sharing her dreams are what inspired my Laundry Room Door.

The Garden Door is just like the door in their rock house that overlooked the Ozark Mountains. The Zinnia Door reminds me of all of the flowers at the old rock house that were tended by several generations of Stockstills. The picture of the house is old, but it looked very much the same way when I first visited Branson. That visit was even written up in the newspaper — I doubt it would be today!

Ice cold watermelon from Hart's Market, shared with my future husband on Table Rock Lake, is the Watermelon Door inspiration. And all of the wildflowers that bloomed in and around that little town of Branson are where the Sunflower Door comes from.

So as you can see, all of the projects in this chapter remind me of Branson — the Branson I knew when my husband I were dating. When birds chirped at dawn and it was a gentler time. There were lots of stars down there, too, back then; only they were all in the night sky.

GRAPEVINE
GARLAND

Intermediate Level

Materials

Two 20"-diameter
    grapevine wreaths
Two 4-oz. bottles glycerine
    (Available at drug stores.)
1 can enamel spray paint, flat black
Two 2-oz. bottles acrylic paint,
    light turquoise
One 2-oz. bottle acrylic paint,
    metallic copper
2 yards 18-gauge wire
Silk and dried decorations:
    2 silk lemons
    1 silk eggplant
    6 silk strawberries
    3 silk ivy garlands
    8 bunches silk grapes with
       wire stems
    12 silk grape leaves
    2 dried stalks okra
    5 dried lotus pods
Exterior varnish, optional

Tools

Pliers
3"-wide paintbrush
Rags

Directions

1. Place both wreaths in bathtub. Fill with enough water to cover wreaths. Add glycerine. I used mixing bowls filled with water to weight down the wreaths. Soak wreaths for 8–12 hours.

2. Remove wreaths from water and cut all bands which are holding the wreaths together. Pull grapevine into desired shape while wet and anchor, if necessary. I used bricks. Allow to dry.

3. Copper-patina the garland and all silk and dried decorations. See "Copper Patina," page 137.

4. Wire all silk and dried decorations to garland.

5. Attach garland to door. See "Attachments," page 139.

Once your basic grapevine garland is completed, you can decorate it for different holidays and seasons. For Christmas, I sprayed dried evergreens and silk poinsettias metallic gold. Then I sprayed them with adhesive and sprinkled them with glitter. I then wired them to the garland. For other holidays, be as creative as you'd like to be. Examples could include adding tulips for springtime, small flags for patriotic holidays, and miniature pumpkins and autumn leaves for fall.

GRAPEVINE
W R E A T H

Intermediate Level

Materials

One 24"-diameter
    grapevine wreath
6 silk grape leaves
1 can enamel spray paint, flat black
Two 2-oz. bottles acrylic paint,
    light turquoise
One 2-oz. bottle acrylic paint,
    metallic copper
3 bunches silk grapes with
    wire stems
One 2-oz. bottle acrylic paint,
    red iron oxide,
    barn red or venetian red
Spray adhesive
1 package gold leaf
$1^1/_2$ yards 18-gauge wire
Exterior varnish, optional

Tools

Pliers
3"-wide paintbrush
Rags

Directions

1. Copper-patina the wreath and silk grape leaves. See "Copper Patina," page 137.

2. Gold-leaf silk grapes. See "Gold Leafing," page 135.

3. Wire leaves in place on wreath.

4. Wire grapes in place on wreath.

If you are placing this wreath on a door where it will be exposed to the elements, it would be a good idea to spray the entire wreath with an exterior varnish.

FLOWER VASES
DOOR

Beginner Level

Materials

One 20" grapevine wreath
4 assorted glass vases
3 yards 1" lace ribbon;
    ivory
3 yards $\frac{1}{4}$" satin ribbon

Tools

Scissors

Directions

1. Cut ribbon into $1\frac{1}{2}$ to 2 foot length, depending on the size of your vase.

2. Tie the ribbons to the wreath with a square knot.

3. Attach the neck of the vase with another square knot.

4. Fill the vases with water and fresh cut flowers.

EASTER
B A S K E T

Intermediate Level

Materials

Basket with handle
Hot glue sticks
Floral foam, to fit basket's base
1 package Easter grass
6 plastic eggs, any variety
2-oz. bottles acrylic paints,
    pink
    light blue
    yellow
    orange
    purple
    white
    dark green
Tracing paper
Carbon paper
$1/8$"-diameter wooden dowel,
    1 yard long
6 small bunches silk flowers
1 yard 2"-wide multicolored
    wired ribbon

Tools

Heavy-duty scissors
Glue gun
Paintbrushes
Pencil
Drill with $1/8$" bit
Saw

Directions

1. Cut basket in half with heavy-duty scissors.

2. Hot-glue floral foam to the inside of basket's base.

3. Cover foam completely with Easter grass and hot glue in place.

4. Paint plastic eggs with a base coat of solid colors. Each egg is a different color.

5. Trace "Egg" pattern onto each egg. See "Stenciling," page 132.

6. Paint eggs according to "Egg" pattern.

7. Drill $1/8$" hole in bottom of each egg.

8. Cut dowel into six 6" lengths.

9. Hot-glue one dowel into each hole.

10. Insert silk flowers and painted eggs into floral foam.

11. Make a bow using wired ribbon and wire. Attach bow to basket handle.

12. Attach basket to door. See "Attachments," page 139.

LAUNDRY
D O O R

Intermediate Level — Laundry Sign
Beginner Level — Clothesline

Materials

Wooden board, 1" x 3" x 15"
One 2-oz. bottle acrylic paint,
    cobalt blue
Tracing paper
Carbon paper
One 2-oz. bottle acrylic paint,
    white
One 2-oz. bottle acrylic paint,
    red
Vinyl clothesline, slightly longer
    than width of your door
12 miniature clothespins
Assorted colors of acrylic paints
Hot glue sticks
Magnets
12 rectangular magnets, $1/4$" x $1/2$"
    (Available at hardware stores.)
6 doll outfits

Tools

#5 flat paintbrush
Photocopy machine
Pencil
#1 round liner paintbrush
Glue gun

Directions

1.   Paint board cobalt blue. Allow to dry.

2.   Using a photocopy machine, enlarge the "Laundry" pattern 125%.

3.   Trace "Laundry" pattern onto painted board. See "Stenciling," page 132.

4.   Paint letters white, then outline each letter with red. Refer to "Laundry" pattern.

5.   Knot clothesline at each end with a simple knot.

6.   Paint each set of clothespins a separate color. You will need two clothespins for each outfit you intend to hang.

7.   Hot-glue magnets to the back of laundry sign. Attach laundry sign to door. See "Attachments," page 139.

8.   Hot-glue small magnets to the back of each clothespin. See "Attachments," page 139.

9.   Hang doll outfits using clothespins from clothesline. The magnets will keep the clothesline in place.

Magnets work great with metal doors. If you do not have metal doors, see "Attachments," page 139.

LAUNDRY
DOOR
PATTERN

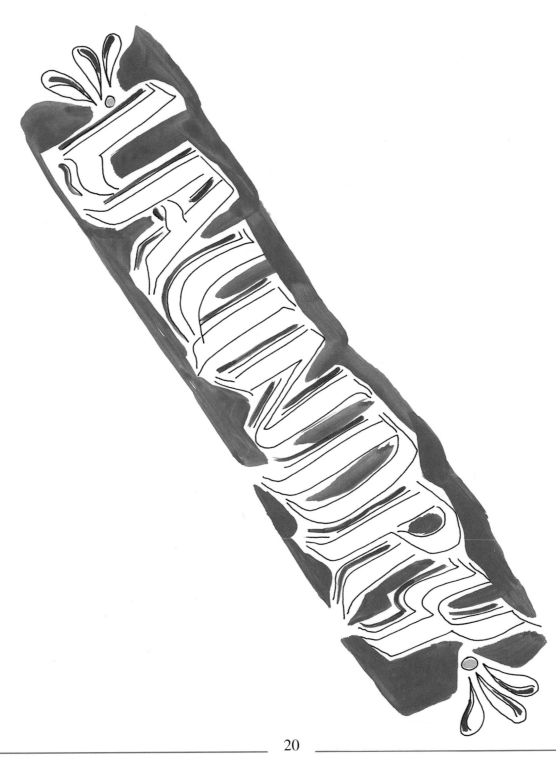

ICE COLD
D O O R

Beginner Level

Materials

4 strips Balsa wood, 3" x 29"
   (To fit across refrigerator door.)
Commercial wood stain or
   antiquing stain
Tracing paper
Carbon paper
2-oz. bottles acrylic paints,
   red
   white
   green
   black
Hot glue sticks
Twenty-four 1" diameter circular
   magnets

Tools

Craft knife
Sandpaper
Photocopy machine
Pencil
#10 flat paintbrush
#3 flat paintbrush
#2 flat paintbrush
Glue gun

Directions

1. Cut Balsa wood into 3" x 29" strips with a craft knife. Sand edges until smooth.

2. Stain strips, applying additional stain to outside edges to give them an antique look.

3. Using a photocopy machine, enlarge the "Watermelon" pattern 200%.

4. Trace "Watermelon" pattern onto strips of Balsa wood. See "Stenciling," page 132.

5. Paint watermelon, except for lettering, according to "Watermelon" pattern. Allow to dry.

6. Trace lettering and paint. Refer to photo for placement.

7. Hot-glue six circular magnets to the back of each wood strip.

8. Attach each wood strip to refrigerator door.

ICE COLD
DOOR
PATTERN

GARDEN
D O O R

Beginner Level

Materials

Door with windows
1 quart acrylic paint,
    white
One 2-oz. bottle acrylic paint,
    green
Mirrors, cut to fit window sections
 	
Tools
 	
2"-wide paintbrush
Sponge
Rags

Directions

1. Paint door white. See "Painting," page 131. Allow to dry.

2. French-wash door with watered-down green acrylic paint. See "Marbleizing: French Wash," page 140.

3. Take door to glass company and have windows replaced with mirrors.

It is easier to paint the door first, then have mirrors installed. Have mirrors put on both sides of the door if both sides show. If your door is an old one, like mine, do not sand or remove old paint first. This gives a truly antique look.

ZINNIAS
DOOR

Intermediate Level

Materials

Kitchen cupboard door
    with glass panes
Tracing paper
Masking tape
2-oz. bottles acrylic paints,
    orange
    red
    yellow
    pink
    white
    blue
    light green
    dark purple
    dark green
    brown

Tools

Pencil
Photocopy machine
Pen and India ink or
    permanent fine-point marker
#2 flat paintbrush

Directions

1. Clean the back side of glass panes. All inking and painting will be done on the back of the glass.

2. Trace the designs on pages 30–33 onto tracing paper. The words will need to be in mirror image. To do this, flip over tracing paper and retrace the same lines. You will need to have a nice, dark copy to follow. Using a photocopy machine, enlarge the "Zinnias" word pattern 125%. All others are actual size.

3. Tape traced design to the **front** of the glass pane with masking tape. This is how your finished project will look. Double-check that your words read correctly. Don't worry about the flowers. It will make no difference if a tendril curls to the left or right; however, you would not want to read "zinnias" backward every morning before you got your coffee cup.

4. Working on the back side of the glass, retrace the design with pen and India ink or permanent fine-point marker. Allow the ink to dry thoroughly.

5. Referring to the patterns, paint as though it were a child's coloring book. You may need to add two or three coats of paint so that the paint is not transparent. Allow each coat to dry thoroughly.

ZINNIAS
DOOR
PATTERNS

ZINNIAS
DOOR
PATTERNS

LATTICE

DOOR

Intermediate Level

Materials

¹/₂ yard fabric, floral pattern or
    enough fabric to cut out the
    desired number of flowers
¹/₂ yard iron-on interfacing
One 2-oz. bottle acrylic paint,
    dark gray
One 2-oz. bottle acrylic paint,
    light green
Wood lattice, 2' x 6'
1 can enamel spray paint, white
4 blocks of wood, 3" x 5" x ³/₄"
8 wood screws, 1¹/₄"
1 can white spray paint
2 silk ivy strands, each 3' long
Hot glue sticks

Tools

Iron
Scissors
2"-wide paintbrush
Screwdriver
Glue gun

Directions

1. Apply iron-on interfacing to fabric according to instructions on package.

2. Cut individual flowers out of fabric.

3. Paint a 2' x 6' section in the middle of the door dark gray. This becomes the background for the lattice.

4. Paint door trim light green.

5. Spray-paint lattice white.

6. Paint the four blocks of wood dark gray.

7. Attach wood blocks to the four corners of the lattice using wood screws.

8. Weave silk ivy in and out of lattice.

9. Attach lattice to door. See "Attachments," page 139.

10. Hot-glue the fabric flowers into place as desired. Refer to photo.

PAINTED
G O U R D S

Intermediate Level

Materials

3 dried gourds
Tracing paper
Carbon paper
2-oz. bottles acrylic paints,
    orange
    light blue
    green
    brown
    black
    white
    pink
    red
12 yards jute or packing twine,
    cut into twelve 1-yard strands

Tools

Photocopy machine
Pencil
Scissors
#6 flat paintbrush

Directions

1. Using a photocopy machine, enlarge the "Apple Trees," "Cow," and "Pumpkins" patterns 125%.

2. Trace the patterns onto gourds. See "Stenciling," page 132.

3. Paint according to patterns. Allow to dry.

4. Take four strands of jute and make even. Tie a knot 3" from one end. Untwist the jute on the 3" side and pull the strands apart to make fringe.

5. Separate the four strands in half and wrap around the narrowest part of the gourd. Tie a knot around the other side of the gourd so that the gourd will look like it has a choker around its neck. Tie another knot at other end of the jute which will tie all four pieces together.

6. Repeat Step 4 for remaining gourds.

7. Combine the final knotted ends of all the strands together by making one big knot. Tie jute around the "necks" of the gourds and tie all strands together with a knot.

8. Hang on a small nail. See "Attachments," page 139.

PAINTED
G O U R D S
P A T T E R N S

HARVEST
PATTERNS

WHEAT
HARVEST

Intermediate Level

Materials

Bundle of dried wheat
    (Approximately 30 stalks.)
1 yard 18-gauge wire
36-gauge copper tooling, 1' x 3'
Tracing paper
Masking tape
One 2-oz. bottle acrylic paint,
    light turquoise
Hot glue sticks

Tools

Pliers
Tin snips or old scissors
Pen, pencil, or copper tool
Stack of paper
Soft cloth
#10 flat paintbrush
Rags
Glue gun

Ribbon Diagram

Directions

1. Tie wheat with wire, making a loop in the back for a hanger.

2. Cut "ribbon" out of copper tooling by cutting a 1" x 36" strip off the long side.

3. Loop ribbon into bow, according to diagram, making a large "M" with long ends. Secure with wire to make a bow.

4. Cut a 1" x 5" strip of copper tooling and center it over the bow's "knot". Refer to photo. This will hide the wire you used to make the bow. Pull edges to back side of copper "ribbon" and fold under with pliers.

5. Trace "Leaf" patterns onto copper tooling. You need one large leaf and two small leaves. Cut and emboss. See "Copper Tooling," page 138.

6. "Age" the center of the leaves by brushing with light turquoise acrylic paint. See "Copper Patina," page 137.

7. Hot-glue leaves and bow to wheat. Refer to photo.

BIRDHOUSE
DOOR

Advanced Level

Materials

1 quart acrylic paint,
  light blue
2-oz. bottles acrylic paints,
  green
  blue
  yellow
  red
  white
  black
  brown
Piece of lumber, 1" x 4" x 6'
Hot glue sticks
$1/4$"-diameter wooden dowel,
  1 yard long
36-gauge copper tooling, 6" x 12"

Tools

2"-wide paintbrush
Pencil
Sponge
Piece of newspaper
Jigsaw or hand saw
Photocopy machine
Drill
$3/16$" drill bit
$1^1/4$" drill bit
Glue gun
Old scissors or tin snips
#6 flat paintbrush

*Standard 4" x 6' cedar fencing
works great for the birdhouses. Or,
if you don't want to fool around
with building a birdhouse, use
prefabricated birdhouses.*

Directions

1. Paint door sky blue. Allow to dry.

2. Lightly pencil in a primitive tree shape on the door. Refer to pattern on page 44. Draw a stick with branches like a child would.

3. Sponge leaves onto tree. See "Marbleizing: Sponging," page 140.

4. From lumber, cut six 8" x 2" side pieces for birdhouses.

5. Using a photocopy machine, enlarge "Bird" and "Birdhouse" patterns 110%.

6. Using a jigsaw or hand saw, cut out three birdhouses. See "Woodcutting," page 142.

7. Drill a $1^1/4$" hole in the front of each birdhouse. Refer to pattern for position.

8. Drill $3/16$" hole for wood perch.

9. For each birdhouse, attach the front to each side with hot glue.

10. Cut three pieces of copper tooling, each 2" x 8". For each, center strip over peak of roof and bend down sides to fit top. Copper will extend slightly beyond sides of birdhouse to form an eave. Hot-glue to top.

11. Cut three 3" dowel sections to make perches. Place hot glue in $3/16$" hole and hammer in dowel.

12. Using jigsaw or hand saw, cut out eight birds. See "Woodcutting," page 142.

13. Paint individual pieces and birds in colors of your choice. Hot-glue all pieces in place on door.

BIRDHOUSE

DOOR

PATTERNS

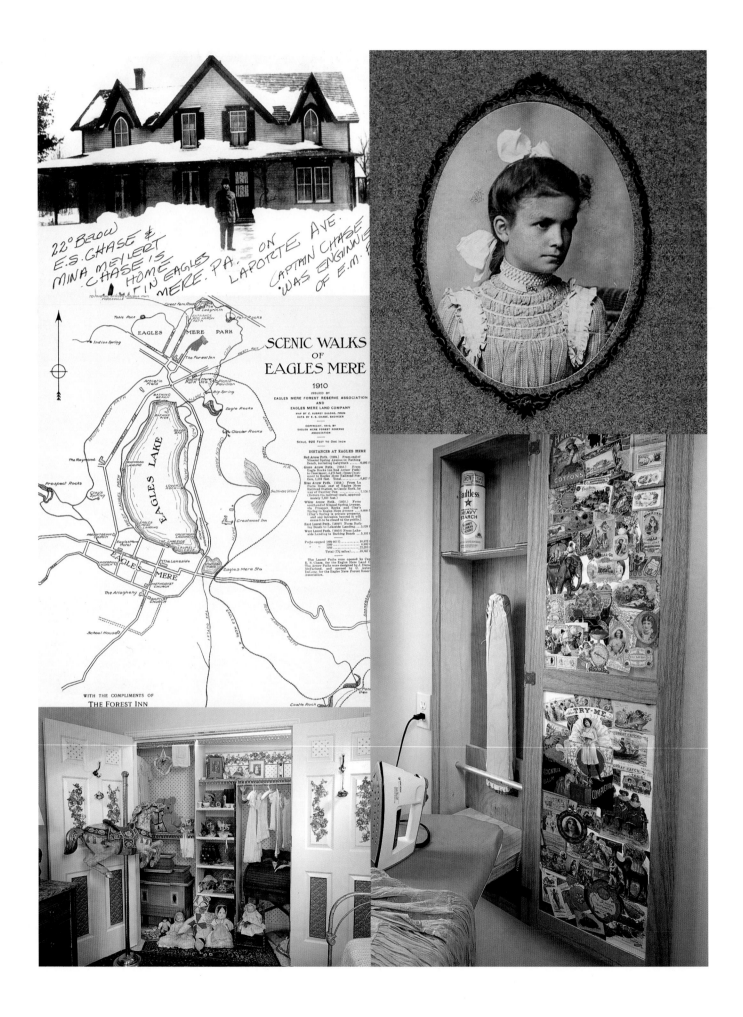

CHAPTER
TWO

Eaglesmere, Pennsylvania

My father was raised by goodly parents and grandparents in Eaglesmere, Pennsylvania, a lake resort area in the Pennsylvania mountains that resonated with elegance and the essence of Victorian charm. The projects in this, the second chapter of my book, were inspired by the memories my father has told me about his mother and his grandfather and by his recollections of Eaglesmere, Pennsylvania.

The slightly pouty young lady in the picture is Edith Chase Hill, my namesake and Grandmother. The picture labeled "22 -below" is her home in Eaglesmere. Look carefully...the door is decorated with an elegant panel of lace, as lovely today as it was back then. This was the inspiration for my lace curtain door.

The map in the picture is one of the maps given by one of the grande olde hotels in Eaglesmere to their guests. The map by the way, was designed by Edith's father, Captain E.S. Chase. He, at one time in his life, was a riverboat captain but he also ran a ferry boat service on Eaglesmere Lake. Looking at his map I can just envision distinguished gentlemen and elegant ladies dressed in yards of cotton organdy and passementier, escaping from the heat of the hot east coast cities to the cool of the mountains.

Eaglesmere reflects a time now gone, but a decorating style that will be much imitated and always loved. It was a time of victorian leisure, of satin, and velvet, and roses, and crystal. A time when decorated doors such as mine with the victorian velvet wreath, the kiosk door, and Sharon's Closet would have been both appreciated and much admired.

SHARON'S
CLOSET

Intermediate Level

Materials

5 yards wallpaper border, large
   floral print
1 double roll small floral print
   wallpaper which
   coordinates with border
1 double roll geometric print
   wallpaper which
   coordinates with border
Temporary flexible adhesive
5 yards tassel fringe
5 yards ¹/₂"-wide lace
5 yards 1"-wide velvet ribbon
Hot glue sticks
Dye remover
Pre-mixed fabric dye,
   2 colors

Tools

Scissors
Glue gun
Drop cloth
Sponge

Directions

1. I antiqued the velvet ribbon for the door first, see "Antiquing Fabric," page 136.

2. Cut individual flowers out of wallpaper border.

3. Cut four small square pieces from small floral print wallpaper to fit the upper panels (two per door).

4. Cut four pieces from the geometric print wallpaper to fit the bottom panels (two per door).

5. Arrange the flowers you have cut from the wallpaper border on the middle panels of each door to create different bouquets. You may temporarily arrange bouquets before permanently pasting them by using temporary flexible adhesive.

6. Following the instructions for applying wallpaper, apply all pieces and flowers to door panels.

7. Cut tassel fringe, lace, and velvet ribbon to fit the edges of the door panels or inner closet shelves. Apply with hot glue.

Keep in mind, you do not have to use ribbons and lace. For instance, a boy's room could have sporting motifs cut out of wallpaper. For a kitchen, you could use fruits and vegetables. Use your imagination!

KIOSK
DOOR

Beginner Level

Materials

Pictures
White glue
Varnish, optional

Tools

Scissors

Directions

1. Cut pictures out of anything.

2. Using white glue, glue pictures to a door in a collage fashion.

There are many great places to find pictures, such as gardening books, magazines, postcards, greeting cards, wrapping paper, ads from antique Victorian magazines, or prints. If you want to decoupage your collage, seal photos with 8 to 12 coats of varnish.

CURTAIN
DOORS

Beginner Level

Materials

His Door:
4 curtain rods with brackets and
    hardware, $^3/_8$" x 28"
    (Adjustable to fit your door.)
$2^1/_2$ yards 44"-wide fabric
1 spool matching thread

Her Door:
2 curtain rods with brackets and
    hardware, $^3/_8$" x 28"
    (Adjustable to fit your door.)
2 curtains, 42" x 6'
2 bows
2 bunches silk flowers

Tools

Screwdriver or hammer
Scissors
Sewing machine

Directions

His Door:

1. Using package instructions, attach curtain rod brackets 6 inches from the top and 6 inches from the bottom of the door.

2. Cut the fabric in half lengthwise along the fold to make two 22"-wide panels.

3. To determine the length of your panels, measure the distance between the rods. Add 6 inches to this measurement to allow for 3 inches on the top and 3 inches on the bottom for $1^1/_2$" rod casings.

4. Finish the long edges by sewing $^1/_4$" seams.

5. Create your $1^1/_2$" rod casings.

6. Place panels on rods and hang.

Her Door:

1. Using package instructions, attach curtain rod brackets 6 inches from the top of the door.

2. Place curtains on rods.

3. You may need to hem curtains to fit door if they are too long.

4. Tie the curtain in the middle with a bow and silk flowers.

HIS
CURTAIN DOORS

HER
CURTAIN DOORS

BANNER
DOOR

Intermediate Level

Materials

1 yard fabric
Matching thread or fabric glue
$1/4$"-diameter wooden dowel,
    18 inches long
Clear acetate
Tracing paper
Carbon paper
Tape
One 2-oz. bottle acrylic paint, black
Paper towels
1 yard black ribbon

Tools

Scissors
Sewing machine, optional
Photocopy machine
Craft knife,
    burning tool or
    single-edged razor
Pencil
Paintbrush

Directions

1. Cut fabric to desired length allowing an extra $1/2$" at bottom for a seam, and an extra 3" on top for a casing. My finished banner is 16" x 35".

2. Finish the left and right sides. To do this, fold $1/4$" to the wrong side of fabric, then fold $1/4$" again. Secure with matching thread or fabric glue.

3. Make a chevron at the bottom of the fabric by finding the bottom center and measuring up 6 inches. Mark this point. Cut in straight line from bottom outside corners to the marked point. Snip $1/2$" straight up from the marked point. Finish the chevron seams in the same manner as for the sides in Step 2.

4. Form a casing for the dowel by folding down $1/4$" of the top of the banner to the wrong side of the fabric. Fold down that seam another $1/2$" so that the $1/4$" seam is inside the $1/2$" seam. Secure with matching thread or fabric glue to form casing.

5. Using a photocopy machine, enlarge "Scroll" pattern 120%. Create a stencil from enlargement. Stencil design onto upper corners of banner. Repeat for bottom corners. See "Stenciling," page 132.

6. On the front of banner, stencil letters down the center, using the "Welcome" pattern.

7. Place banner on dowel. Tie a ribbon to each end of dowel.

8. Attach to door. See "Attachments," page 139.

BANNER
DOOR
PATTERNS

VELVET
WREATH

Intermediate Level

<table>
<tr><td>

Materials

One 16"-diameter straw wreath
1 yard velvet fabric
Dye remover
Pre-mixed fabric dyes,
    country blue and wine
Hot glue sticks
3 plastic roses with leaves
Acrylic paint, color for
    base coat of crackle finish
Hide glue or crackle-finish craft glue
Acrylic paint, color for
    top coat of crackle finish
Spray varnish
One 2-oz. tube artist oil color,
    burnt umber
Paint thinner
Oil-based varnish
9 yards ⅛" ribbon, any light color

Tools

Tape measure
Scissors
Drop cloth
Sponge
Glue gun
2"-wide paintbrushes
Rags or old paintbrush
Plastic gloves

</td></tr>
</table>

Circumference

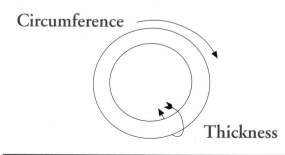

Thickness

Directions

1. Using a tape measure, measure around outside circumference of wreath, then cut velvet twice as long. Measure around the thickness of the wreath; just like you are measuring your waist (see diagram below). This measurement plus one inch will be the width of your fabric.

2. Antique the velvet. See "Antiquing Fabric," page 136. I started with navy blue velvet and removed color with dye remover to a silvery gray.

3. Lay fabric along front side of wreath. Gather as necessary. Pull sides together, adjust gathers so they are even, and secure with hot glue.

4. If possible, take rose petals and leaves off wire so that you can paint each individually.

5. Crackle-finish the roses. See "Crackle Finish," page 134.

6. Antique the roses. See "Antiquing," page 133. Reassemble roses and glue.

7. Cut ribbon into 1-yard lengths. Divide into three bundles. Place the first bundle of ribbons on top of each other and tie them around wreath into a bow. Repeat with remaining bundles. See photo for placement. Note: I dyed the ribbons to match the velvet.

8. Hot-glue roses on top of bows.

CHAPTER
THREE
Salt Lake City, Utah

This third chapter is me: a blend of old and new, of plain and fancy, of reality and fantasy. My decorative style has been called eclectic, but I like to think of it as a collage of all of the different places that I have lived, loved, and been influenced by.

When my husband and I were just married, we moved to Springfield, Missouri. Our daughter, Sharon, was born there. Soon we found ourselves moving across Kansas and our son Steve was born in Wichita. The screen door you will find in this chapter reminds me of all of those midwest homes and the many friends that welcomed me in. (Hi Susie. Hi Dorothy. Yes, I actually have a friend in Kansas named Dorothy!)

We lived in Arizona for several years, and I loved everything about it. The country cut out door with cactus and the snakes is one that was greatly influenced by my love of the Arizona desert. The little

lizard on the kitchen cupboard door reminds me of the tiny lizards that lived in my garden and scooted across our walls.

We now live in Salt Lake City and Door with a View was photographed across the street from my house. In the background are the majestic Wasatch Mountains that I have come to love as much as the midwest and the desert. The Flowerbox Door was influenced by my love of flowers and my Salt Lake garden and the second country cut out door with the geese and the cows reflects my love of country primitive folkart. This door is in my studio where, when not in my garden, I spend most of my time.

I love pets as much as I do flowers - even the friendly lizards that lived on our walls in Arizona. Because of this I had to include at least one door that you might not think of as very important or worth decorating - your pet door. That is where Ollie's Door came from. So, as you can see, the doors in Chapter 3 are all of me!

SOLEIL·

SUN & STARS
DOOR

Intermediate Level

Materials

2 oz. bottles acrylic paints,
    white
    dark blue
    rust
    gold
    terra cotta
    beige
Newspaper
36-gauge copper tooling, 12" x 24"
Tracing paper
Masking tape
Hot glue sticks
100–150 assorted plastic gemstones
50 plastic stars
One 2-oz. tube artist oil color,
    white
Paint thinner
Oil-based varnish

Tools

2"-wide paintbrush
#10 flat paintbrush
#1 round liner paintbrush
Sponge
Photocopy machine
Pen, pencil, or copper tool
Stack of paper
Soft cloth
Tin snips or old scissors
Glue gun
Rags or old paintbrush
Plastic gloves

Directions

1. Paint door white. See "Painting," page 131. Allow to dry.

2. Paint trim dark blue.

3. Paint small trim rust.

4. Sponge and marbleize center panel with gold and terra cotta. See "Marbleizing: Sponging," page 140.

5. Using a photocopy machine, enlarge the "Sun" pattern 200%.

6. Trace "Sun" pattern onto the sheet of copper tooling. Cut and emboss. See "Copper Tooling," page 138.

7. Hot-glue onto door.

8. Hot-glue gemstones around edges of door and glue stars in an "S" pattern around the sun. Refer to photo.

9. Whitewash entire door including copper and gemstones. See "Antiquing," page 133.

SUN & STARS
DOOR
PATTERN

BATHROOM
DOOR

Intermediate Level

Materials

2 oz. bottles acrylic paints,
    white
    dark blue
    rust
    gold
    terra cotta
    beige
Newspaper
Door knocker
Particle board, 2' x 4'
Tracing paper
Carbon paper
Tape
Hot glue sticks

Tools

2"-wide paintbrush
#10 flat paintbrush
#1 round liner paintbrush
Sponge
Pencil
Table saw or jigsaw
Glue gun

Directions

1. Paint door white. See "Painting," page 131. Allow to dry.

2. Paint trim dark blue.

3. Paint small trim rust.

4. Sponge and marbleize center panel with gold and terra cotta. See "Marbleizing: Sponging," page 140.

5. Paint trim on mirror (and matching trim for inside bathroom) dark blue.

6. Cut individual triangular particle board "tiles" that measure $3^1/2$" x $3^1/2$" x $4^1/2$". The number of tiles needed may vary depending on the size of your door. My door was $80^1/2$" from top to bottom and 30" wide. See "Woodcutting," page 142.

7. Paint "tiles" terra cotta.

8. Mount door knocker on the door.

9. Hot-glue painted tiles into place. Refer to photo.

10. Whitewash entire door. See "Antiquing," page 133, or "Marbleizing: French Wash," page 140.

The bathroom was painted to coordinate with the door and hallway. The bathroom cabinet was marbleized gold and the wall trim was whitewashed blue, like the trim on the doors. I painted the whole hall, pantry door, and bookcase to match. I included a photo so that you could see the entire area!

SCREEN
D O O R

Intermediate Level

Materials

Screen door, black
Knob and back plate
Tracing paper
Clear acetate
Newspaper or drop cloth
One 2-oz. bottle acrylic paints,
    white
    black
DMC cross-stitch floss,
    754 Peach-lt.
    761 Salmon-lt.
    760 Salmon
    320 Pistachio Green-med.
    356 Terra Cotta-med.
1 can enamel spray paint, flat black
Two 2-oz. bottles acrylic paint,
    light turquoise
One 2-oz. bottle acrylic paint,
    metallic copper
Silk ivy garland, 3 feet
1/8"-wide ribbon,
    pale peach, 3 yards
    pale pink, 3 yards
    mauve, 3 yards
8 satin roses
Hot glue sticks

Tools

Craft knife, burning tool or
    single-edged razor
Paintbrush
#26 tapestry needle for cross-stitching
3"-wide paintbrush
Rags
Glue gun

Directions

1. Create a stencil from the letters provided for the "Banner Door," see page 61. See "Stenciling," page 132.

2. Remove screen door, place over newspaper or drop cloth. Arrange letters in a slight arch pattern and stencil with white paint. Allow to dry. Remove stencils and touch up mistakes with black paint.

3. Cross-stitch roses onto screen door. See cross-stitch grid on the following page. Refer to photo.

4. Patina knob. See "Copper Patina," page 137. Attach knob and back plate to the center panel of door according to package instructions or hot glue in place.

5. Twist garland into a circle, approximately 14" in diameter. Place three ribbon lengths on top of each other and tie into a large bow. Wrap around wreath. Hot-glue satin roses onto wreath. Refer to photo.

6. Hang the garland from the knob with one of the ribbon loops.

SCREEN
DOOR
CROSS-STITCH GRID

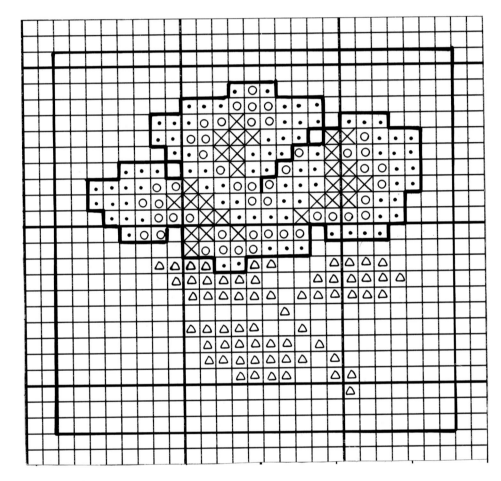

Anchor   **DMC (used for sample)**

Step 1: Cross-stitch (2 strands)

4146	·	754 Peach-lt.
8	○	761 Salmon-lt.
9	✕	760 Salmon
215	△	320 Pistachio Green-med.

Step 2: Backstitch (1 strand)

5975		356 Terra Cotta-med.

DOOR
WITH A VIEW
PATTERN

DOOR
WITH A VIEW

Advanced Level

Materials

Door without panels
Window frame with glass
Print or poster to fit window
Shutters to fit window
1 quart flat acrylic paint, lime green
Construction-strength wood glue
Countersunk wood screws or
    plastic anchors and toggle
2-oz. bottles acrylic paints,
    red
    pale yellow
    dark green
    blue
Hide glue or
    crackle-finish craft glue
2-oz. bottles acrylic paints for crackle,
    black, red
Spray varnish
Four 2" hinges with hardware
Shoe box
Tracing paper
Carbon paper
Tape
Hot glue sticks
Floral foam, cut to fit shoe box
Spanish moss
Silk plants

Tools

2"-wide paintbrush
#10 flat paintbrush
#1 round liner paintbrush
Screwdriver
Photocopy machine
Pencil
Glue gun

Directions

1. Paint door lime green. See "Painting," page 131. Allow to dry.

2. Apply wood glue to outside edges of print or poster and attach to the back of the window frame.

3. Using countersunk wood screws (if you have a solid wood door) or plastic anchors and toggle (if you have a hollow core door), attach window frame to door. You may be able to use construction-strength wood glue. See "Attachments," page 139.

4. To achieve an antique look on the shutters, I used a crackle finish. See "Crackle Finish," page 134. Paint shutters black first, then paint red on top.

5. Attach shutters with hinges to the sides of the window frame according to the instructions that came with the hinges.

6. Paint shoe box pale yellow.

7. Using a photocopy machine, enlarge "Floral" pattern 125%. Trace pattern onto shoe box. See "Stenciling," page 132. Paint according to pattern.

8. Hot-glue floral foam inside shoe box. Hot-glue Spanish moss over foam.

9. Hot-glue shoe box under window frame.

10. Insert silk plants into the floral foam.

 # ANGEL
DOOR

Beginner Level

Materials

3 pre-cast resin angels
One 2-oz. bottle acrylic paint,
    red iron oxide,
      barn red, or venetian red
Spray adhesive
1 package gold leaf
Whitewash, optional
Exterior varnish, optional
$2^1/_2$ yards 3"-wide
    metallic gold ribbon
4 small nails
3 sawtooth hangers

Tools

#10 flat paintbrush
Hammer

Directions

1. Gold leaf angels. See "Gold Leafing," page 135.

2. Tie metallic gold ribbon in a bow.

3. Hang ribbon with a small nail on door. Refer to photo.

4. Hang angels using sawtooth hangers and small nails on top of the ribbon. Refer to photo. See "Attachments," page 139.

FLOWER
BOXES

Beginner Level

Materials

To make one flower box:
Shoe box
1 can enamel spray paint, flat black
Two 2-oz. bottles acrylic paint,
    light turquoise
One 2-oz. bottle acrylic paint,
    metallic copper
Tracing paper
Carbon paper
Tape
Hot glue sticks
Floral foam, cut to fit shoe box
Spanish moss
Silk plants

Tools

3"-wide paintbrush
Rags
Pencil
Ice pick
Glue gun

Directions

1. Patina shoe box. See "Copper Patina," page 137. Allow to dry.

2. Trace "Heart" pattern onto shoe box. See "Stenciling," page 132.

3. Following the lines of the pattern, punch through the shoe box with an ice pick at approximately $1/4$" intervals.

4. Hot-glue floral foam inside shoe box. Hot-glue Spanish moss over foam.

5. Insert silk plants into the floral foam.

FLOWER
BOXES
PATTERNS

Using a photocopy machine, enlarge pattern 135%.

OLLIE'S
DOLLHOUSE &
SUMMER DOORS

Beginner Level

Materials

Dollhouse Door:
3 strips Balsa wood,
    size depends on size of door
One 2-oz. bottle acrylic paint,
    white
Temporary adhesive gum
Hot glue sticks
Knickknacks for decoration

Hand-Painted Door:
Tracing paper
Carbon paper
Tape
2-oz. bottles acrylic paints,
    pink
    green
    blue

Tools

Tape measure
Pencil
#1 round liner paintbrush
Craft knife
Sandpaper
#10 flat paintbrush
Glue gun
Photocopy machine

*Keep in mind that small
knickknacks at pet-door level
are not suitable for homes
with small children.*

Directions

Dollhouse Door:

1. Measure door opening. Using a craft knife, cut Balsa wood into strips slightly longer than measurements to frame the door opening. Sand edges until smooth.

2. Paint wood strips white.

3. Using temporary adhesive gum, attach wood strips around door opening to create a frame.

4. Hot-glue knickknacks onto wood strips.

Summer Door:

1. Using a photocopy machine, enlarge pattern 125%. Trace pattern around pet door. See "Stenciling," page 132.

2. Hand-paint according to photo.

OLLIE'S
SUMMER DOOR
PATTERN

OLLIE'S
CHRISTMAS DOOR
PATTERNS

OLLIE'S
CHRISTMAS DOOR

Beginner Level

Materials

3 strips Balsa wood,
    size depends on size of door
One 2-oz. bottle acrylic paint,
    red
Tracing paper
Carbon paper
Tape
One 2-oz. bottle acrylic paint,
    green
One 2-oz. bottle acrylic paint,
    white
Temporary adhesive gum
1" lumber
Hot glue sticks
Knickknacks for decoration

Tools

Tape measure
Craft knife
Sandpaper
#10 flat paintbrush
Photocopy machine
Pencil
Jigsaw
#1 round liner paintbrush
Glue gun

Directions

1. Measure door opening. Using a craft knife, cut Balsa wood into strips slightly longer than measurements to frame the door opening. Sand edges until smooth.

2. Paint wood strips red.

3. Using a photocopy machine, reduce or enlarge pattern to desired size; then trace onto wood strips. See "Stenciling," page 132.

4. Paint strips according to photo.

5. Using temporary adhesive gum, attach wood strips around door opening to create a frame.

6. Using a photocopy machine, enlarge "Christmas Tree" pattern 125%. Trace pattern onto 1" lumber twice. See "Stenciling," page 132.

7. Using a jigsaw, cut Christmas Trees out. See "Woodcutting," page 142.

8. Paint as desired.

9. Using temporary adhesive gum, place Christmas trees to each side of the door.

10. Hot-glue knickknacks onto wood strips.

PUMPKIN

DOOR

Beginner Level

Materials

3-foot grapevine garland
36-gauge copper tooling, 12" x 24"
Tracing paper
Carbon paper
Tape
One 2-oz. bottle acrylic paint,
    orange
One 2-oz. bottle acrylic paint,
    tan
1-oz. tube artist oil color,
    burnt umber
1 oz. paint thinner
1 oz. oil-based varnish
Hot glue sticks

Tools

Photocopy machine
Pen, pencil, or copper tool
Stack of paper
Soft cloth
Tin snips or old scissors
#10 flat paintbrush
Rags
Plastic gloves
Glue gun

Directions

1. Using a photocopy machine, take the "Pumpkin" pattern below and make one copy at 100% and four enlargements — you choose the sizes you prefer. Trace the five "Pumpkin" patterns. See "Stenciling," page 132.

2. Trace all "Pumpkin" patterns onto the sheet of copper tooling. Cut and emboss. See "Copper Tooling," page 138.

3. Paint pumpkins orange with tan stems.

4. Antique pumpkins. See "Antiquing," page 133.

5. Hot-glue painted pumpkins in place on garland. Refer to photo.

COUNTRY
C U T O U T S

Advanced Level

Materials

2-oz. bottles acrylic paints,
    pale yellow
    blue
    white
    red
    black
    green
6 linear feet of lumber, 1" x 12"
Tracing paper
Carbon paper
Tape
Hot glue sticks
Magnets, 1"

Tools

2"-wide paintbrush
Photocopy machine
Pencil
Jigsaw
Glue gun

Directions

1. Paint door, excluding raised panels, pale yellow. Paint the center panels blue and sponge with white paint. Paint the beveled edges on the sides red. If door has no panels, create fake panels by masking off sections with masking tape and painting them different colors. See "Painting," page 131.

2. Using a photocopy machine, enlarge "Cow" patterns 115%, enlarge both "Duck" patterns 125%, and enlarge "Heart" pattern 135%. Trace patterns onto wood. See "Stenciling," page 132.

3. Using a jigsaw, cut traced shapes out. See "Woodcutting," page 142.

4. Paint cutouts according to pattern and photo. If desired, antique. See "Antiquing," page 133.

5. Hot-glue magnets to the backs of each cutout. Hang cutouts on door. Refer to photo. See "Attachments," page 139.

COUNTRY
CUTOUTS
PATTERNS

COUNTRY
CUTOUTS
PATTERNS

SOUTHWEST
CUTOUTS
PATTERNS

SOUTHWEST
CUTOUTS

Advanced Level

Materials

2-oz. bottles acrylic paints,
 red
 blue
 yellow
 white
 black
 green
6 linear feet of lumber, 1" x 12"
Tracing paper
Carbon paper
Tape
Hot glue sticks
Magnets, 1"

Tools

2"-wide paintbrush
Photocopy machine
Pencil
Jigsaw
Glue gun

Directions

1. Paint door, excluding raised panels, pale yellow. Paint the center panels blue and sponge with white paint. Paint the beveled edges on the sides red. If door has no panels, create fake panels by masking off sections with masking tape and painting them different colors. See "Painting," page 131.

2. Using a photocopy machine, enlarge "Cactus" and "Star" patterns 150%. "Snake" pattern is actual size. Trace patterns onto wood. See "Stenciling," page 132.

3. Using a jigsaw, cut traced shapes out. See "Woodcutting," page 142.

4. Paint cutouts according to pattern and photo. If desired, antique. See "Antiquing," page 133.

5. Hot-glue magnets to the backs of each cutout. Hang cutouts on door. Refer to photo. See "Attachments," page 139.

CREATURE
DOOR

Beginner Level

Materials

Plastic toy,
        frog, dinosaur, etc.
Temporary adhesive gum
Tracing paper
Carbon paper
Tape
Lightweight cardboard, 6" x 6"
2-oz. bottles acrylic paints,
        red
        turquoise
        yellow
        white
        black

Tools

Pencil
Scissors
#5 flat paintbrush
#2 round liner paintbrush
Photcopy machine

Directions

Lizard Door:

1. Using a photocopy machine, enlarge "Lizard" pattern to 125%. Trace the pattern onto lightweight cardboard. See "Stenciling," page 132.

2. Using scissors, cut lizard out.

3. Paint lizard's body red. Allow to dry.

4. Using the pattern you have already traced, place lizard's body detail on cardboard lizard and paint. Refer to photo.

5. Using temporary adhesive gum, attach the lizard to your door. See "Attachments," page 139.

Plastic Toy Door:

Using temporary adhesive gum, attach plastic creature to your door. Now is that easy enough or what?!!

 # AMOIRE
DOOR

Advanced Level

Materials

1-quart acrylic paint,
    dark blue
2-oz. bottles acrylic paints,
    yellow
    red
    black
    dark green
    white
    turquoise
    gold
    burgundy
    coral
    purple
    tan
    brown
    peach
    orange
Tracing paper
Carbon paper
Tape
One 2-oz. tube artist oil color,
    burnt umber
Paint thinner
Oil-based varnish

Tools

2"-wide paintbrush
#10 flat paintbrush
#2 round liner paintbrush
Photocopy machine
Pencil
Rags or old paintbrush
Plastic gloves

Directions

1. Paint the outer trim of the doors dark blue.

2. Paint the inside center panels yellow.

3. Paint a 1" border of red around the yellow center panels.

4. Paint each corner of this red border black.

5. Paint the remaining areas dark green, shading each corner on the diagonal. Refer to photo.

6. Paint the middle areas between the panels white. This is where I hand-letter the saying: *"Happiness should always be with you. It should always bloom and never wither."*

7. Using a photocopy machine, enlarge all patterns 125%. Trace and transfer the patterns. See "Stenciling," page 132.

8. Paint the "Basket of Flowers" pattern on the top and bottom of each door. I varied each bouquet slightly to add interest — for example, add a pear instead of the grapes, and change the color of the flowers and fruit.

9. Freehand-paint added detail such as monograms, striping, scrolls, and words. Refer to photo.

10. Antique entire doors. See "Antiquing," page 133.

AMOIRE
DOOR
PATTERN

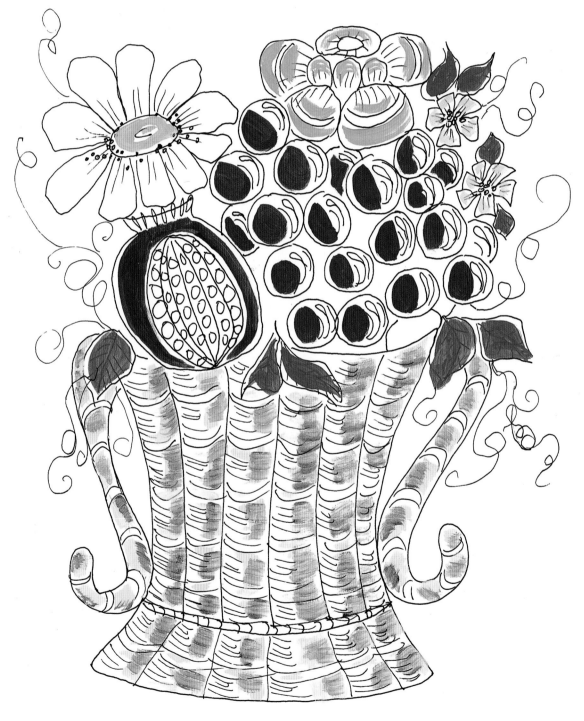

HIDDEN
DOOR KNOCKER
PATTERN

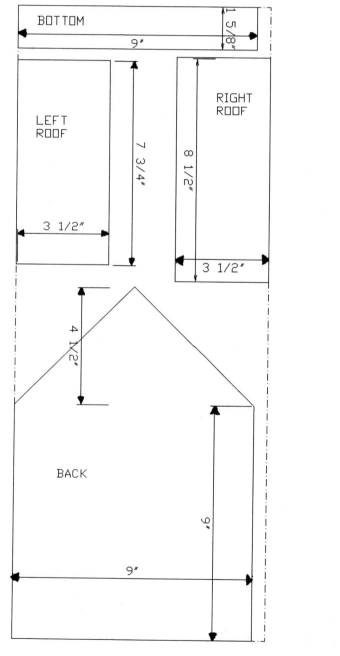

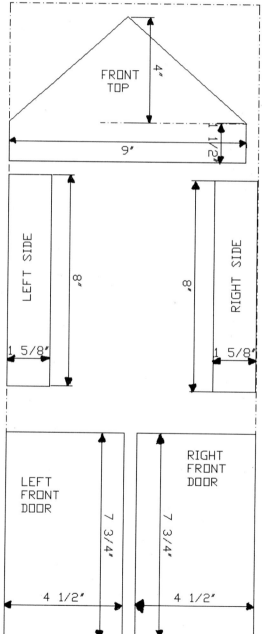

HIDDEN

D O O R K N O C K E R

Advanced Level

Materials

4 linear feet of lumber, 1" x 10"
   (White pine works well.)
Tracing paper
Carbon paper
Tape
2-oz. bottles acrylic paints,
   green
   red
   blue
   yellow
Door knocker with hardware
12 wood screws, $1^{1}/_{4}$"
Wood putty
4 utility hinges, $1^{1}/_{2}$"
2 brass knobs, 1"
Hot glue sticks
20 magnets, 1"

Tools

Pencil
Tape measure
Jigsaw or table saw
Screwdriver or drill
Sandpaper
#10 flat paintbrush
Glue gun

Directions

1. Lay out wood according to diagram.

2. Cut out wood with jigsaw or table saw. See "Woodcutting," page 142.

3. Miter top of roof at a 45-degree angle.

4. Paint each piece the desired color before assembling. Refer to photo.

5. Attach door knocker to the inside back of house according to package directions.

6. Using wood screws, assemble the house. First, attach the bottom and sides to the back. Next, attach the top front piece; then the two roof pieces.

7. After the house is assembled, fill the screws with wood putty. Allow putty to dry. Sand and touch up paint.

8. Attach the two front doors using the utility hinges. Attach brass knobs.

9. Hot-glue magnets to the back of the house. Attach to door. See "Attachments," page 139.